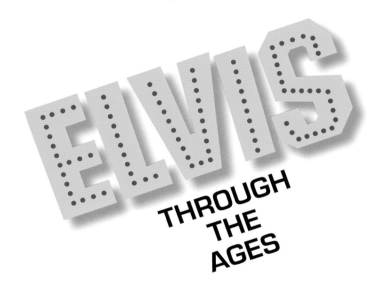

ELVIS

THROUGH THE AGES

ELVIS
THROUGH THE AGES

IMAGES FROM THE HOLLYWOOD PHOTO ARCHIVE

CAPTIONS AND COMMENTARY BY **BOZE HADLEIGH**

LP

LYONS
PRESS

Guilford, Connecticut

An imprint of The Rowman & Littlefield Publishing Group, Inc.
4501 Forbes Blvd., Ste. 200
Lanham, MD 20706
www.rowman.com

Distributed by NATIONAL BOOK NETWORK

British Library Cataloguing in Publication Information available

Library of Congress Cataloging-in-Publication Data available

ISBN 978-1-4930-3349-2 (hardcover)
ISBN 978-1-4930-4097-1 (e-book)

∞™ The paper used in this publication meets the minimum requirements of American National Standard for Information Sciences—Permanence of Paper for Printed Library Materials, ANSI/NISO Z39.48-1992.

This is dedicated to Ronald Boze Stockwell and to the memory of Flora and Walter.

—B.H.

BY THE SAME AUTHOR:

Marilyn: Lost Images from the Hollywood Photo Archive
Marilyn Forever
Elizabeth Taylor: Tribute to a Legend
Hollywood Gays
Hollywood Lesbians: From Garbo to Foster
Celebrity Feuds!

CONTENTS

ABOUT THE HOLLYWOOD PHOTO ARCHIVE

The Hollywood Photo Archive is not only a wonderful collection of cinematic history, it captures the collective memories of Hollywood. The gunmen, the gallants, the ghosts and the stars of the big screen are represented in an impressive archive of more than 180,000 pieces.

The collection has been assembled over forty years by Director Colin Slater. In Slater's early days, as he began to learn his craft, it was the great directors, Wilder, Lean, and Welles, who advised him to study and learn from the film stills. Slater went on to own an important public relations agency, The Adventurers, in association with the legendary journalist and film executive, Fred Hift. Together with 500 stringers the company worked on almost every motion picture produced and released in the U.K., gathering stills from the stars and press collateral from the studios. Added with Hift's lifetime of files the Hollywood Archive was born.

The outstanding archive provides a treasure trove of prints for film buffs; delve in and discover wonderful film stills, celebrity portraits and heroic stage performances. For more information contact wkdirections@outlook.com.

Part 1:
Young Elvis

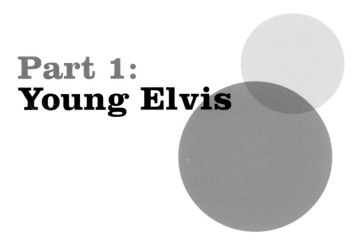

Elvis Aron Presley was born in Tupelo, Mississippi, on January 8, 1935, half an hour after twin brother Jessie (sic) Garon Presley, who was born dead. Mother Gladys often told her surviving only child that he'd inherited the other's life force and was special. Elvis and his doting, often worried mother grew very close, for father Vernon was often away seeking work. The family lived in near-constant poverty.

Elvis was split between a need to conform—later legally amending his middle name to the more standard Aaron—and to stand out. In school he was periodically asked to cut his hair and he sported then-daring sideburns, even penciling them in before they grew in. Innately musical, his singing was a comfort when better-dressed kids at school shunned him. As a grown-up Elvis wouldn't wear blue jeans and didn't like people around him to wear denim, which symbolized hard times and derision.

In 1948 Elvis and his parents moved to Memphis, Tennessee. "Dad packed all our belongings in boxes and put them on the top and in the trunk of a 1939 Plymouth." The Presleys and four relatives of Gladys settled into one house with one bathroom. Again, music helped the youth transcend his surroundings.

At family and other gatherings young Elvis inevitably sang and eventually wanted a guitar to accompany himself. Or a gun. Gladys dissuaded him from the gun by helping him save up enough for a guitar. The instrument became his constant companion, even when he became a truck driver. One trucker boss prophetically declared Elvis would have to pick between music and trucking.

Elvis the singer-guitarist and bandmates Scotty Moore and Bill Black sought work wherever they could find it, traveling in and out of Tennessee. In time they became well known through much of the South. Teenagers in particular responded to Elvis's uninhibited intensity and spontaneous physical energy, what one critic termed "shaky hips and itchy legs" and many parents called obscene.

Presley opted for full-time music soon after his trio was contracted by *Louisiana Hayride*, a popular Saturday night show out of Shreveport, LA, to appear weekly for a year. For driving the seven-hours from Memphis to Shreveport every week, Elvis earned $18 per appearance and the two men $12 each. Elvis's popular act became each show's finale. Elvis's very last appearance on *Louisiana Hayride* was the first time an announcement was made, to calm the excited and still-expectant fans, that "Elvis has left the building."

The singer's very first record, in summer 1953, was one he bankrolled. For about four dollars he recorded "My Happiness" and "That's When Your Heartaches Begin." He gave the record to his mother as a present. It was made at the Memphis Recording Service, which later became Sun Records. Hoping for work, Elvis informed office manager Marion Keisker that he enjoyed singing all sorts of music. Following his session, she made a note: "Good ballad singer. Hold."

Sun owner Sam Phillips waited until late 1954 to contact Elvis. He was seeking a white singer who had "the sound and feel" of a black musician. Keisker suggested the boy whose unusual name Phillips couldn't remember. "The kid with the sideburns," he ordered. Keisker phoned young Presley and according to one biographer "when she called, Elvis literally ran all the way to the studio, arriving out of breath while she was still holding the phone."

However, Elvis's first commercial recording wasn't released, and there were assorted pre-stardom disappointments. One of the worst was after he got to appear at Nashville's country-music haven, the Grand Old Opry, and was reportedly advised by its director he should return to truck driving. But Elvis was already moving from "hillbilly" and country music to rock 'n roll and rhythm-and-blues.

It was rock and teen reaction—and over-reaction—to Elvis Presley's looks and overtly sexy (very un-1950s) performances and the resultant controversy and publicity that soon catapulted him to national and international fame. He'd gradually widened his musical arenas from rural and Southern to the teenagers' rock to, eventually (in the '60s), ballads and music for all ages. The king of rock 'n roll became, during and after his movie career, the king of pop, outselling all other singers before and since. ✳

▼ ELVIS ARON PRESLEY, CIRCA 1942. HE LATER LEGALLY CHANGED HIS MIDDLE NAME TO AARON, CHOOSING THE MORE COMMON SPELLING.

▲ ELVIS ARON PRESLEY IN 1941 OR '42 (DEPENDING ON THE SOURCE) IN HIS HOMETOWN OF TUPELO, MISSISSIPPI.

▶ ELVIS PRESLEY'S HUMBLE CHILDHOOD HOME IN TUPELO, MISSISSIPPI, SINCE PAINTED WHITE, IS NOW A MUSEUM. THE FAMILY WAS FORCED TO MOVE OUT A FEW YEARS AFTER ELVIS'S BIRTH DUE TO LACK OF PAYMENT.

▼ NOTICE HOW MIDDLE-AGED MOST TEENAGERS LOOKED IN THE 1950S: ELVIS PRESLEY'S PHOTO IN THE 1953 YEARBOOK OF HUMES HIGH SCHOOL IN MEMPHIS, TENNESSEE. HE COULDN'T JOIN THE FOOTBALL TEAM UNLESS HE CUT HIS "LONG HAIR."

PHILLIPS, JAMES ARNETT
Major: Science, Special Studies, Drafting, English.
Activities: Thespian, National Forensic, Debate Team, Spanish Club, Hi-Y, Biology Club, History Club, Speech Club, Student Council Representative, Non-Com Officer in R. O. T. C., Vice-President Speech Club, Vice-President History Club.
Awards: Winner District Debate Tournament, Winner "I Speak For Democracy" Contest.

ROBINSON, KATIE MAE
Major: Commercial, Home Ec., English.
Activities: F. H. A., History Club, English Club, Vice-President History Club.

RULEMAN, SHIRLEY
Major: Home Ec., Commercial, English.
Activities: National Honor Society, F. H. A., Y-Teens, Latin Club, Jr. Cheerleader, Sabre Club, History Club, English Club, Honorary Captain in R. O. T. C., President Home Ec. Class.

PRESLEY, ELVIS ARON
Major: Shop, History, English.
Activities: R. O. T. C., Biology Club, English Club, History Club, Speech Club.

PERRY, ROBERT EARL
Major: History, Science, English.
Activities: Biology Club, T&I Club, Key Club, Baseball 4 years, Vice-President Key Club, Boys' Vice-President Senior Class, President T&I Club.
Awards: All-Star American Legion Baseball Team 1952, National Honor Society.

SANDERS, MARY LOUISE
Major: Commercial, Band, English.
Activities: Senior Band, Y-Teens, English Club, History Club, Historian of Band.

SEALY, CAROLYN NAOMI
Major: Commercial, Art, English.
Activities: Fifty Club, Y-Teens, Red Cross, Monitor, Sight-Saving Room.
Award: Merit Award in Lion Oil Essay Contest, Scholastic Golden Key Award in Art.

ROTENBERRY, JAMES RUSSELL
Major: Drafting, Shop, English.
Activities: History Club, English Club, Biology Club, Hi-Y Science Club, President Science Club, Vice-President Biology Club.

ROBINSON, EDWARD McMILLAN
Major: Math, Drafting, English.
Activities: Biology Club, History Club, Rifle Team, English Club, Student Council Representative.

SEXTON, BONNIE
Major: Commercial, Home Ec., English.
Activities: F. H. A., Y-Teens, Red Cross, Student Council, Honor Society, Herald Staff, Secretary F. H. A., Vice-President Red Cross, Secretary Senior Class.
Awards: Attended F. H. A. Convention in Nashville.

SLATE, SHIRLEY
Major: Commercial, English.
Activities: English Club, History Club, Y-Teens, Glee Club.

RICE ROBERT
Major: Drafting, Art, English.
Activities: R. O. T. C., English Club, History Club, T&I Club.

▲ ELVIS SINGING HIS HEART OUT IN TAMPA, FLORIDA, IN JULY 1955, ACCOMPANIED BY HIS NEW MARTIN D-28 GUITAR. THIS PHOTO APPEARED ON THE COVER OF HIS FIRST ALBUM, ELVIS PRESLEY, RELEASED IN 1956 (HIS PANTS' KNEES ARE DIRTY DUE TO ELVIS'S HABIT OF SLIDING TO HIS KNEES ONSTAGE).

◀ IN 1954 ELVIS AND HIS BAND BEGAN PERFORMING AT THE *LOUISIANA HAYRIDE*, A WEEKLY SHOW OUT OF SHREVEPORT THAT LAUNCHED SEVERAL COUNTRY SINGERS. THE TRIO WAS INVITED BACK EVERY SATURDAY NIGHT FOR A YEAR, MAKING THE SEVEN-HOUR DRIVE FROM MEMPHIS TO SHREVEPORT—ELVIS EARNED $18 PER SHOW, HIS BANDMATES $12 EACH.

▲ ELVIS AND SAM PHILLIPS, THE HEAD OF HIS RECORD LABEL, IN 1956 AT SUN STUDIOS. PHILLIPS, WHO FOUNDED SUN RECORDS AND HELPED LAUNCH SEVERAL SINGERS, WAS A RECORD PRODUCER, EXECUTIVE, AND DJ. HE WAS INSTRUMENTAL IN POPULARIZING ROCK 'N ROLL IN THE 1950S.

▶ THIS JANUARY 1955 PHOTO WAS SELECTED BY COLONEL PARKER FOR ELVIS'S FANS AND WAS USUALLY SIGNED. THE "COLONEL" LATER REVEALED THAT ELVIS DIDN'T AUTOGRAPH PHOTOS AND SCOLDED ANYONE NAÏVE ENOUGH TO THINK THAT HE DID.

▲ SUN RECORDS, OWNED AND OPERATED BY
SAM C. PHILLIPS, BECAME NATIONALLY KNOWN
FOR LAUNCHING SEVERAL MEMPHIS-AREA
ARTISTS, INCLUDING ELVIS, ROY ORBISON,
JERRY LEE LEWIS, JOHNNY CASH, CARL PERKINS,
AND B.B. KING.

On the photo (handwritten): To Virginia your Friend Carl Perkins

Dear Virginia,
God Loves us all.
Johnny Cash

SUN RECORD COMPANY

◄ AN EXUBERANT ELVIS IN 1955, A YEAR OF HIGHS AND SOME LOWS. AFTER PERFORMING AT NASHVILLE'S GRAND OLE OPRY ITS DIRECTOR REPORTEDLY TOLD PRESLEY HE SHOULD RETURN TO DRIVING A TRUCK. THE SHOW'S HEADLINER, "HILLBILLY COMIC" ANDY GRIFFITH, LATER NOTED, "THE OPRY WAS PRETTY TRADITIONALIST AND DIDN'T REALLY CATER TO THE YOUNG PEOPLE."

▲ ON DECEMBER 4, 1956, AT SUN RECORDS STUDIO IN MEMPHIS, ELVIS JOINED JERRY LEE LEWIS (LEFT) AND CARL PERKINS FOR WHAT BECAME KNOWN AS THE "MILLION DOLLAR QUARTET" ALTHOUGH JOHNNY CASH (RIGHT) WAS PRESENT FOR THE PICTURE-TAKING ONLY.

► POSTER FOR TWO MEMPHIS CONCERTS ON SUNDAY, FEBRUARY 6, 1955, INCLUDING "MEMPHIS' OWN" ELVIS PRESLEY AND BANDMATES SCOTTY (MOORE) AND BILL (BLACK). "HE'LL SING 'HEARTBREAKER' AND 'MILK COW BOOGIE.'"

◄ EARLY DURING HIS HOLLYWOOD CAREER ELVIS MET SEVERAL MOVIE STARS (IN THIS CASE NATALIE WOOD IN MEMPHIS IN OCTOBER 1956). HE LATER PREFERRED TO HOLD COURT WITH HIS "MEMPHIS MAFIA" RATHER THAN SOCIALIZE WITH FELLOW CELEBRITIES.

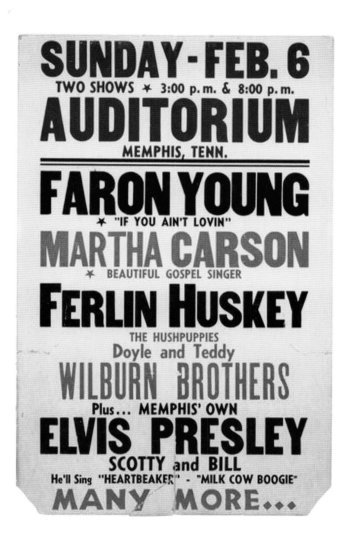

▶ YULETIDE AT HOME IN MEMPHIS, 1957, THE YEAR OF ELVIS'S CHRISTMAS ALBUM. MANY THOUGHT IT OBSCENE FOR ELVIS TO RECORD RELIGIOUS SONGS AND THE ALBUM WAS BOYCOTTED BY SEVERAL RADIO STATIONS. COMPOSER IRVING BERLIN WASN'T PLEASED WITH PRESLEY'S RENDITION OF HIS SONG "WHITE CHRISTMAS."

▼ YOUNG ELVIS WANTED TO SAVE UP AND BUY A GUN BUT MOTHER GLADYS STRONGLY PREFERRED HE BUY A GUITAR TO ACCOMPANY HIS SINGING; SHE HELPED HIM PURCHASE ONE AND IT BECAME A CONSTANT COMPANION AND SECURITY BLANKET.

20th
CENTURY-FOX
presents

RICHARD
EGAN
DEBRA
PAGET
and introducing
ELVIS
PRESLEY
in

Love Me
Tender

CINEMASCOPE

CO STARRING
ROBERT MIDDLETON · WILLIAM CAMPBELL · NEVILLE BRAND
with MILDRED DUNNOCK · BRUCE BENNETT   PRODUCED BY DAVID WEISBART · DIRECTED BY ROBERT D. WEBB · SCREENPLAY BY ROBERT BUCKNER · BASED ON A STORY BY MAURICE GERAGHTY

◀ SOON AFTER TOM PARKER ARRANGED FOR A
SCREEN TEST WITH PRODUCER HAL WALLIS,
ELVIS BOWED ON SCREEN IN *LOVE ME
TENDER* (1956), ORIGINALLY TITLED THE RENO
BROTHERS (PRESLEY PLAYED THE YOUNGEST
OF FOUR). IT WAS RETITLED FOR THE SONG
ELVIS SINGS AT FADEOUT AFTER HE'S DIED.

▶ ELVIS'S SECOND MOVIE, *LOVING YOU* (1957),
PROVED HIS SCREEN STARDOM WASN'T A
FLUKE. IN 1956 IT WAS A TOSS-UP WHETHER
HIS SINGING STARDOM WOULD TRANSLATE
TO MOVIES. THUS, RICHARD EGAN AND DEBRA
PAGET WERE BILLED ABOVE HIM IN *LOVE ME
TENDER*. FROM 1957 ON, ELVIS WAS ALWAYS
FIRST-BILLED.

▲ NEITHER ELVIS NOR HIS MANAGER KNEW
WHETHER THE PRESLEY CAREER WOULD
OUTLAST ELVIS'S TWO-YEAR STINT IN THE
ARMY, SO TOM PARKER HAD HIM RECORD
NUMEROUS SONGS BEFORE HIS 1958
INDUCTION FOR RELEASE DURING THE
SINGER'S ABSENCE TO KEEP ELVIS'S VOICE AND
MEMORY FRESH AMONG THE PAYING PUBLIC.

◀ RUSSIAN BALLET STAR RUDOLPH NUREYEV
SAID, "PRESLEY MOVES LIKE A NATURAL
DANCER . . . HE CANNOT SING STANDING
STILL, HIS ENERGY NEEDS EXPRESSION." HERE,
ELVIS IS VIRTUALLY EN POINTE—THE BALLET
TERM FOR ON THE TIPS OF THE TOES—IN
JAILHOUSE ROCK (1957).

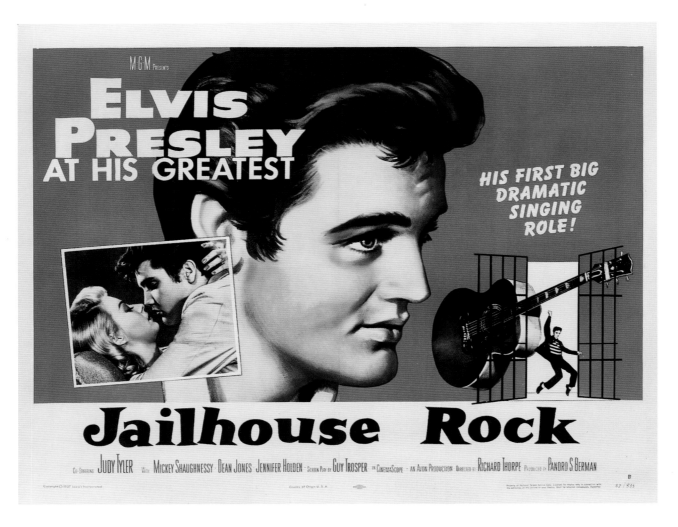

▲ DAUGHTER LISA MARIE'S FAVORITE OF HER FATHER'S FILMS IS *JAILHOUSE ROCK* (1957) BECAUSE IT SHOWCASED HIM AS A REBEL.

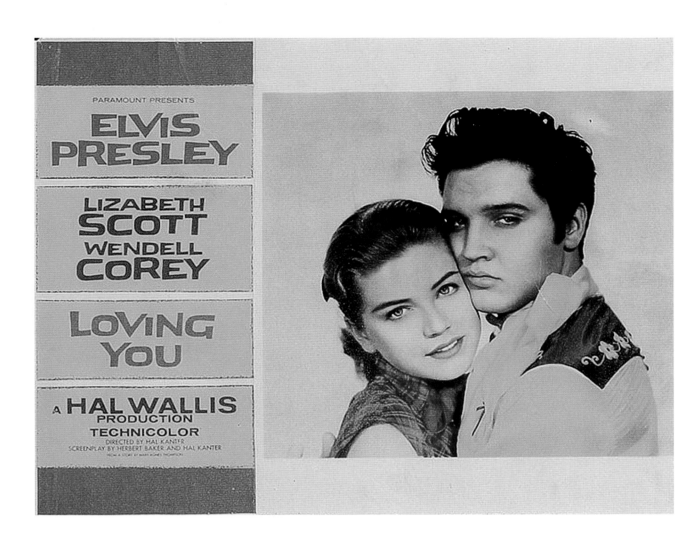

PARAMOUNT PRESENTS

ELVIS PRESLEY

LIZABETH
SCOTT
WENDELL
COREY

LOVING
YOU

A HAL WALLIS
PRODUCTION
TECHNICOLOR
DIRECTED BY HAL KANTER
SCREENPLAY BY HERBERT BAKER AND HAL KANTER
FROM A STORY BY MARY AGNES THOMPSON

◀ ELVIS ATTENDED LAS VEGAS PERFORMANCES BY
LIBERACE, A FAVORITE OF GLADYS PRESLEY, IN
APRIL AND NOVEMBER, 1956. AFTER THE SECOND
SHOW THE MEN SOCIALIZED BACKSTAGE AND
POSED FOR PHOTOGRAPHERS.

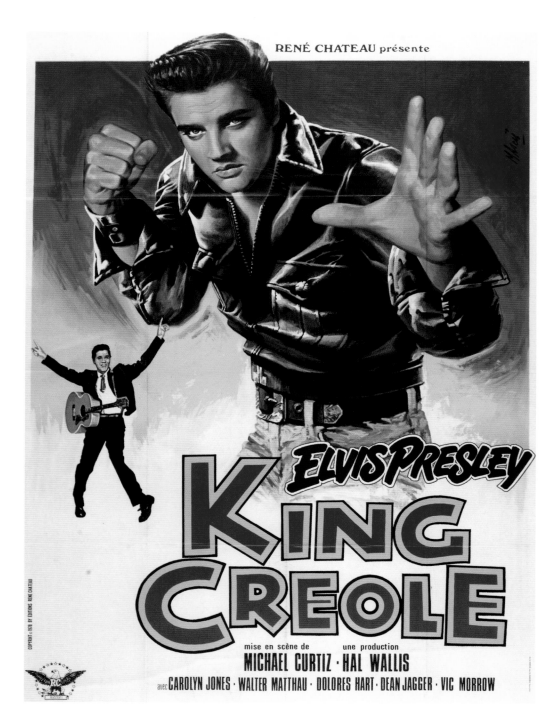

RENÉ CHATEAU présente

ELVIS PRESLEY
KING CREOLE

mise en scène de   une production
MICHAEL CURTIZ · HAL WALLIS

avec CAROLYN JONES · WALTER MATTHAU · DOLORES HART · DEAN JAGGER · VIC MORROW

▲ ELVIS ENJOYED THE FACT THAT *KING CREOLE* (1958) WAS ORIGINALLY INTENDED AS A JAMES DEAN VEHICLE (THE TITLE REFERS TO A NIGHTCLUB, NOT AN INDIVIDUAL).

10216-NPS-C/1

▲ NEITHER SOPHIA LOREN NOR ELVIS PRESLEY
FELT MUCH AT HOME IN HOLLYWOOD.
IN 1958 THEY MET IN THE PARAMOUNT
COMMISSARY, WHERE THE ITALIAN MOVIE STAR
TOLD HIM, "I BET YOU WISH THEY WOULD
STOP SCREAMING" (PHOTOGRAPHER BOB
WILLOUGHBY WAS ON HAND AND TOOK A
SERIES OF PLAYFUL PICTURES).

◀ ELVIS'S *KING CREOLE* (1958) COSTAR CAROLYN
JONES NOTED, "WHEN ELVIS WAS NEW TO
ACTING HE AND HIS MANAGER WEREN'T SURE
OF THEMSELVES AND LET THE MOVIEMAKERS
BE BOSS. . . . OURS WAS HIS FOURTH FILM, THE
LAST BEFORE HE WAS DRAFTED. AFTER THAT,
THE MOVIES GOT CHURNED OUT MORE OFTEN
AND WITH LESS QUALITY."

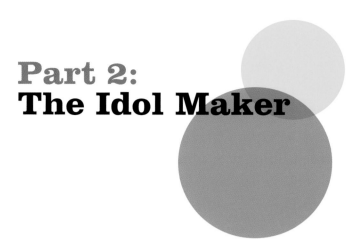

Part 2:
The Idol Maker

The real name of Elvis's manager Colonel Tom Parker (1909–1997) was Andreas Cornelis (sic) van Kuijk. He was an illegal alien, a secret which Elvis Presley never knew though it significantly impacted his career. Van Kuijk entered the United States in 1929, perhaps through Canada, and may or may not have killed a woman in his native Holland, which he seems to have fled of necessity.

The non-colonel found work in carnivals. One carnie act was "Colonel Parker's Dancing Chickens," a hot plate sprinkled with sawdust atop which birds hopped to keep from getting burned, to the tune of "Turkey in the Straw." Another scheme was painting sparrows yellow and selling them as canaries.

Later, Parker managed country singer Eddy Arnold, who finally fired the domineering Colonel. When Parker came upon Elvis in 1955 he remarked the twenty-year-old's good looks, his gullibility, and his potential. Parker studied the singer's impact on audiences more closely than he studied Elvis, whose music wasn't the Dutchman's type. Elvis already had a manager and was contracted to Sun Records but the Colonel moved in as a "special advisor," then replaced the manager, then decided Sun was too limited a record label and got RCA to take over the contract.

Parker had first had to win over the minor's parents. Gladys Presley mistrusted him and after he explained in detail his gold-plated plans for Elvis, her first question was what church denomination Parker belonged to? Mr. Presley was more easily lured. In 1937 Vernon, who worked as a sharecropper, a milkman, a carpenter, and a general laborer, was arrested for changing the amount on a four-dollar check. He served eight months in prison and was released early as a "hardship case."

When Parker provided lucrative musical employment for Elvis—whose billing was sometimes misspelled Alvis—the youth, who took pride in helping support his family, was delighted. His pre-Parker goal had been to join a well-known band. It didn't happen. He recorded "Without You" for Sun founder Sam Phillips. It didn't get released. Yet Phillips was impressed enough to keep Elvis on and teamed him with talented musicians Scotty Moore, a guitar player, and Bill Black, a bass player. The trio rehearsed for Phillips until they developed their own style. On July 5, 1954, they recorded "That's All Right," Elvis's first hit.

Radio listeners demanded more Elvis and later that month he performed his first concert, as the opening act for country singer Slim Whitman. By December he was successful enough to get a manager, Tom Neal. By 1955 it was clear that Elvis had a big future, as a solo act. But where Phillips and Neal had predicted Southern stardom for their client as the king of country music, Tom Parker—perhaps due to a foreigner's eye—saw national and international stardom for Elvis Presley.

Parker, a shrewd negotiator as well as promoter, won over Elvis as his lifelong client via the RCA recording contract that led to television that led to Hollywood in 1956. The latter gave Elvis his widest and most lucrative fame, but movies, or the Colonel's take-the-money-and-run choice of movies, eventually ran Elvis's career into the ground. With the early-'60s British invasion, especially the Beatles, Elvis was no longer king of the charts and during his screen heyday garnered no #1 hits.

By 1969 Elvis's movies were widely considered a joke, and he quit acting. The Colonel engineered a big comeback via television, followed by a musical film documentary. Demand for in-person Elvis soared, and he conquered Las Vegas and began the extended hotel dates and concert tours that lasted the rest of his life. Tom Parker ran Presley's career to the end, cutting himself in for fifty percent of the take and making secret side deals his client didn't know about. He failed to give Elvis important tax breaks because of his near-paranoid fear of possible interaction with the US government. As an illegal alien Parker was potentially liable to deportation.

Despite huge demand for Elvis to sing in Europe, Japan, and elsewhere, the Colonel routinely declined all non-US offers. Elvis only did three foreign concerts, in Canada in 1957. Parker didn't accompany him. The man who routinely accompanied "my boy," as he called him, had no passport or US citizenship. Had he somehow been able to enter another country with Elvis Presley, "Tom Parker" wouldn't have been allowed back into the United States. ✳

Colonel Parker & Elvis

▲ TOM PARKER, WHO'D PREVIOUSLY MANAGED SINGER EDDIE ARNOLD (WHO FIRED HIM) NEVER ALLOWED ELVIS TO PERFORM OUTSIDE THE US, DESPITE TREMENDOUS DEMAND. HAD THE "COLONEL" SOMEHOW BEEN ABLE TO LEAVE THE US, HE WOULDN'T HAVE BEEN ALLOWED BACK IN. (THIS SPRING 1966 PHOTO WAS TAKEN ON THE SET OF *SPINOUT* (1966).)

▶ THE REAL NAME OF NON-COLONEL TOM PARKER, ELVIS PRESLEY'S STORIED MANAGER AND PROMOTER, WAS ANDREAS CORNELIS (SIC) VAN KUIJK, AN ILLEGAL DUTCH IMMIGRANT WHO EVENTUALLY POCKETED FIFTY PERCENT OF HIS CLIENT'S INCOME— WITH ELVIS'S CONSENT.

COLONEL PARKER'S BRAINCHILD FOR HIS "GOLDEN BOY," THE FAMOUS GOLD SUIT, WAS WORN SELDOM IN 1957 (ELVIS FELT HE LOOKED "CLOWNISH" IN IT) BUT MADE THE 1959 ALBUM COVER OF 50,000,000 ELVIS FANS CAN'T BE WRONG. PARKER COMPLAINED THAT GOLD WAS FLAKING OFF AT THE KNEES EVERY TIME ELVIS GOT DOWN ON THEM DURING HIS "HOUND DOG" CONCERT FINALE—SO ELVIS TRADED THEM FOR BLACK PANTS AND SOON DROPPED THE ENTIRE OUTFIT.

KING OF ROCK 'N ROLL: ORIGINALLY IDENTIFIED WITH REGIONAL (SOUTHERN) AND COUNTRY MUSIC, ELVIS WASN'T ALWAYS EAGER TO LABEL HIMSELF MONARCH OF A MUSICAL GENRE THAT THROUGH MUCH OF THE 1950S WAS FIERCELY CONDEMNED IN THE PRESS, IN PULPITS, AND BY PARENTS AS IMMORAL AND A MENACE TO AMERICAN YOUTH.

The King Of Rock n Roll

COLONEL PARKER PIONEERED CELEBRITY MERCHANDISING, LICENSING MYRIAD ELVIS PRODUCTS, FROM LAMPS AND LIPSTICK TO CHARM BRACELETS AND HANDKERCHIEFS TO GUITARS AND GLOW-IN-THE-DARK BUSTS. 1956 SALES OF SUCH ITEMS TOTALED A THEN-IMPRESSIVE $22 MILLION.

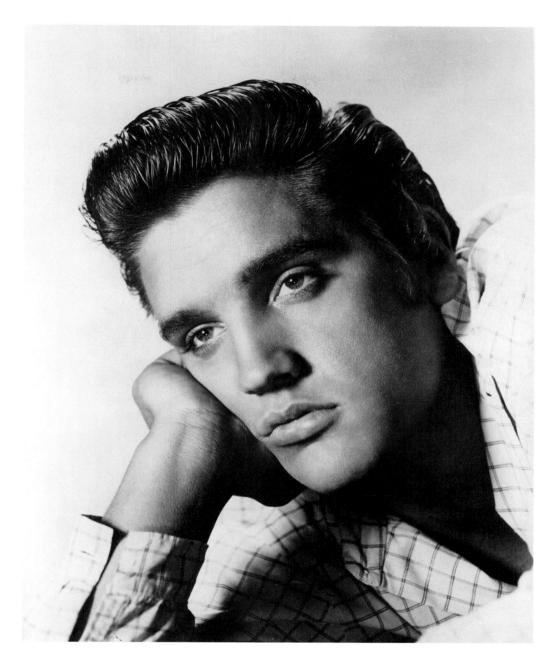

◄ ELVIS WASN'T ALLOWED TO GIVE A FREE
CONCERT FOR ARMY TROOPS AFTER HE GOT
DRAFTED IN 1958. THE COLONEL ORDERED,
"IF THEY WANT MY BOY TO SING, THEY ARE
GOING TO HAVE TO PAY FOR IT LIKE ANYONE
ELSE."

▲ "LOVE ME TENDER," THE TITLE SONG OF ELVIS'S
1956 SCREEN BOW, WAS A RE-WORDED CIVIL
WAR BALLAD TITLED "AURA LEE" (AKA "AURA
LEA"). A RECORDING IN HIS 1969 FLICK *THE
TROUBLE WITH GIRLS—AND HOW TO GET INTO
IT* USED THE SAME MELODY BUT MORPHED
INTO "VIOLET (FLOWER OF NYU)."

▲ ELVIS MET FUTURE WIFE PRISCILLA ANN
BEAULIEU, STEPDAUGHTER OF A US AIR
FORCE CAPTAIN, WHILE HE WAS STATIONED
IN GERMANY. PRESLEY WAS TWENTY-FOUR,
PRISCILLA WAS FOURTEEN . . . SHE WAS
GROOMED TO BE HIS EVENTUAL WIFE, WHEN
HE WAS READY AND WHEN THE COLONEL
WAS (HE FEARED FANS WOULD DESERT A
MARRIED ELVIS).

◄ PRIVATE ELVIS PRESLEY (A SERGEANT UPON HIS
DISCHARGE IN 1960) WAS OFTEN DEPRESSED
AND LONELY DURING HIS TWO YEARS IN
THE ARMY, SPENT MOSTLY IN GERMANY. ELVIS
BELIEVED HIS BEST DAYS WERE BEHIND HIM,
PROFESSIONALLY, AND WASN'T ALWAYS
LIKED BY MORE PRIVATE AND LESS PUBLICIZED
PRIVATES.

▶ ALTHOUGH ELVIS, SEEN HERE IN *G.I. BLUES* (1960), FEARED THAT BEING DRAFTED WOULD END HIS BURGEONING CAREER, IT IN FACT PLEASED AND REASSURED MANY ESTABLISHMENTARIANS AND PLACED HIM MORE FIRMLY IN THE MAINSTREAM.

▼ SERGEANT ELVIS PRESLEY HOLDS A PRESS CONFERENCE IN GERMANY (THE COLONEL'S IDEA) IN MARCH 1960 BEFORE RETURNING HOME FROM THE ARMY. NOTICE THE PROMINENT BLONDE FRAULEIN.

▲ ELVIS IS BACK: IN THE USA AGAIN, SGT. PRESLEY
HOLDS A PRESS CONFERENCE (STAGED BY
GUESS WHO) AT FORT DIX, NEW JERSEY, IN
MARCH 1960 SHORTLY BEFORE HIS DISCHARGE
FROM THE ARMY.

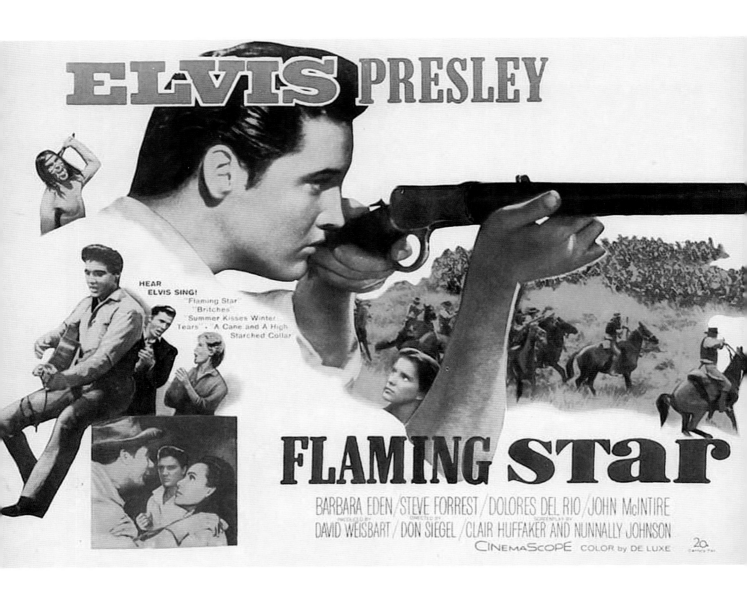

ELVIS PRESLEY

HEAR ELVIS SING!
"Flaming Star"
"Britches"
"Summer Kisses Winter Tears" · "A Cane and A High Starched Collar"

FLAMING STAR

BARBARA EDEN / STEVE FORREST / DOLORES DEL RIO / JOHN McINTIRE
PRODUCED BY DAVID WEISBART / DIRECTED BY DON SIEGEL / SCREENPLAY BY CLAIR HUFFAKER AND NUNNALLY JOHNSON
CINEMASCOPE   COLOR by DE LUXE

▲ MEXICAN MOVIE STAR DOLORES DEL RIO PLAYED ELVIS'S NATIVE AMERICAN MOTHER IN *FLAMING STAR* (1960), HIS SECOND POST-ARMY FILM AND A NON-MUSICAL. AS A "HALF-BREED" HE IS FORCED TO SIDE WITH THE "INDIANS" AFTER WESTERN SETTLERS SHOOT HIS MOTHER.

WILD IN THE COUNTRY (1961) WAS ABOVE-AVERAGE ELVIS FARE ABOUT A RURAL DELINQUENT WITH LITERARY TALENT BUT LIMITED EDUCATION, TORN BETWEEN FUN-TIME GIRL TUESDAY WELD AND MILLIE PERKINS WHO URGES HIM TOWARD COLLEGE—ALSO HOPE LANGE AS A PSYCHIATRIC CONSULTANT TRYING TO REHABILITATE HIM.

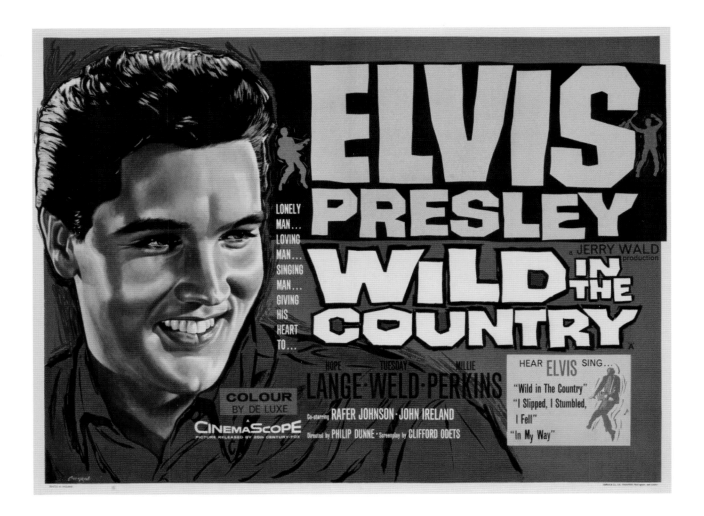

▼ ELVIS SERENADES JOAN BLACKMAN WITH A
UKULELE IN **BLUE HAWAII** (1961), ONE OF HIS
MOST SUCCESSFUL MOTION PICTURES.
A LATER ISLANDS-THEMED MOVIE, **PARADISE—
HAWAIIAN STYLE** (1966), HAD NOWHERE THE
SAME SUCCESS.

▲ ELVIS GOES HAWAIIAN: HE SINGS TO LOCAL ACCOMPANIMENT IN **BLUE HAWAII** (1961), WHOSE SOUNDTRACK ALBUM WAS ELVIS'S MOST SUCCESSFUL AND ONE OF HIS BEST— AND INCLUDED MORE SONGS (FOURTEEN) THAN ANY OTHER OF HIS MUSICAL SOUNDTRACKS.

ANGELA LANSBURY (NOT SEEN IN PHOTO!) PLAYED ELVIS'S MOTHER IN **BLUE HAWAII** (1961): "MAMA WANTS ELVIS TO GO INTO THE FAMILY PINEAPPLE BUSINESS. HE WANTS TO BE A TRAVEL GUIDE. GUESS WHO WINS? . . . ELVIS TOLD ME I SOUNDED MORE SOUTHERN THAN HE EVER DID."

ONE OF THE MOST MEMORABLE SCENES IN ELVIS'S THIRTY-ONE FILMS WAS THE CLIMACTIC BOAT WEDDING SCENE, SET TO MUSIC OF COURSE, IN **BLUE HAWAII** (1961)—ELVIS MARRIES JOAN BLACKMAN AND THEY PLAN TO OPEN THEIR OWN TRAVEL AGENCY.

◀ THOUGH **KID GALAHAD** (1962) CAST ELVIS AS A
BOXER, IT WAS THE USUAL FORMULA VEHICLE OF
MOSTLY FORGETTABLE SONGS, UNMEMORABLE
ACTRESSES, AND REDUNDANT (NON-BOXING)
FISTICUFFS, ALL APPROVED BY THE COLONEL FOR
MAXIMUM PROFIT, INCLUDING THE INEVITABLE
SOUNDTRACK RECORD ALBUM.

▼ IN **FOLLOW THAT DREAM** (1962, WITH JOANNA
MOORE) ELVIS PLAYED "SORT OF A HAPPY-GO-
LUCKY BEACH BUM WHO SINGS AND LIKES KIDS,"
SAID DIRECTOR DAVID WEISBART. "IN REALITY,
ELVIS ISN'T THAT HAPPY-GO-LUCKY. BUT HE'S
INTERESTED IN MARTIAL ARTS AND IN OUR MOVIE
HE USES IT [JUDO] TO FEND OFF THE BAD GUYS."

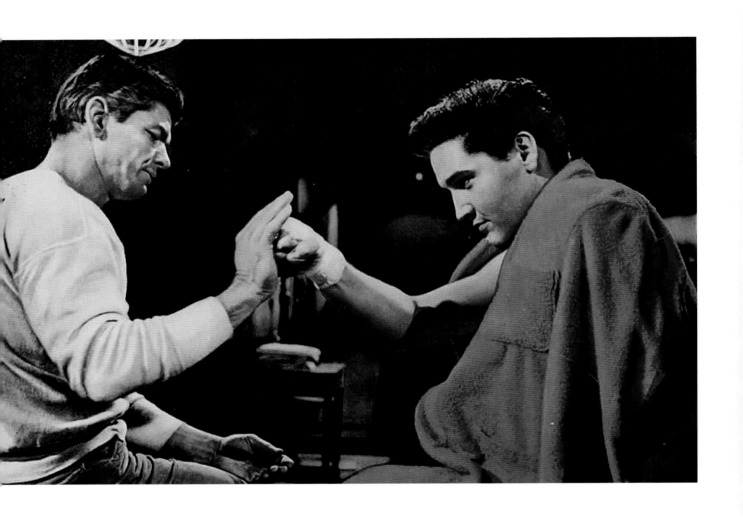

▶ SEEING EYE TO EYE: IN *IT HAPPENED AT THE WORLD'S FAIR* (1963) PILOT ELVIS WINS NURSE JOAN O'BRIEN AFTER THE BIG MISUNDERSTANDING THAT TEMPORARILY IMPEDES ROMANCE IN THE TYPICAL ELVIS VEHICLE (THE PAIR LUNCHES AT SEATTLE'S BRAND-NEW SPACE NEEDLE, CONSTRUCTED FOR THE FAIR).

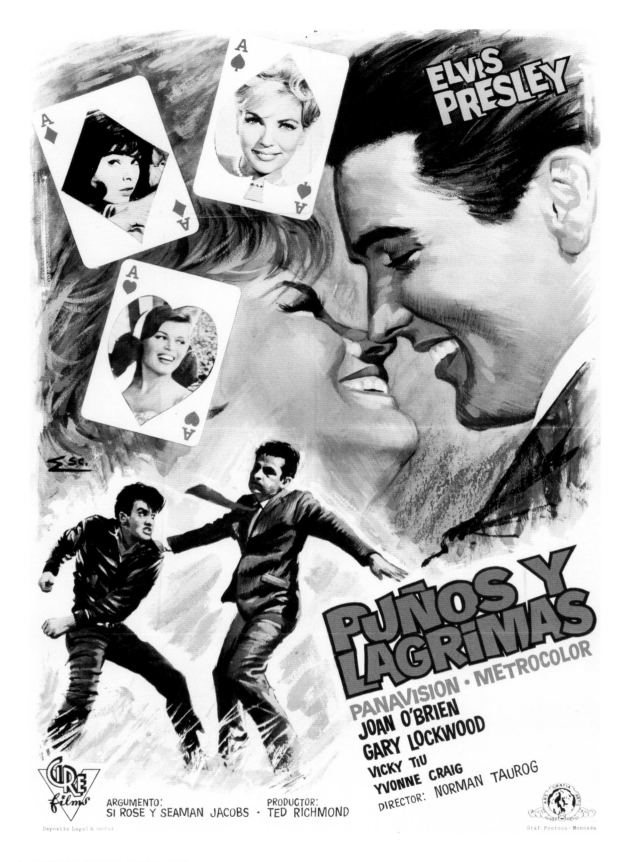

◀ **PUÑOS Y LAGRIMAS** (FISTS AND TEARS)
WAS THE SPANISH-LANGUAGE TITLE OF **IT
HAPPENED AT THE WORLD'S FAIR** (1963),
WHICH CASHED IN ON THE MASSIVE PUBLICITY
SURROUNDING THE SEATTLE WORLD'S FAIR.

▲ ADMIRING THE HAM: IN SEPTEMBER 1962
IN SEATTLE, ELVIS WAS PRESENTED WITH A
HAM BY WASHINGTON GOVERNOR ALBERT
ROSELLINI (LEFT), WHILE COL. PARKER (RIGHT)
AND NORMAN TAUROG, DIRECTOR OF **IT
HAPPENED AT THE WORLD'S FAIR** (1963),
LOOK ON.

▼ ELVIS, WHO ESCHEWED BLUE JEANS, WAS
SENSITIVE ABOUT BEING PERCEIVED AS A HICK
AND FELT AMBIVALENT ABOUT *KISSIN' COUSINS*
(1964), IN WHICH HE PLAYED LOOK-ALIKES, ONE A
HICKISH STEREOTYPE.

▲ THE ONLY TIME ELVIS APPEARED BLOND ONSCREEN WAS AS JODIE (WHOSE LOOK-ALIKE, JOSH, HAS THE REGULATION BLACK HAIR) IN *KISSIN' COUSINS* (1964). JODIE ROMANCES A BLONDE WAC PLAYED BY CYNTHIA PEPPER.

▶ ELVIS MOVIES USUALLY LACKED IMPORTANT ROMANTIC COSTARS. ANN-MARGRET OF *VIVA LAS VEGAS* (1964) WAS HIS MOST PROMINENT LEADING LADY; THE PAIRING YIELDED THE MOST FINANCIALLY SUCCESSFUL OF ALL HIS FILMS. IN 1975 COL. PARKER TORPEDOED ELVIS'S COSTARRING WITH BARBRA STREISAND IN HER 1976 HIT REMAKE OF *A STAR IS BORN*.

▲ **LOVE IN LAS VEGAS** WAS THE UK TITLE OF **VIVA LAS VEGAS** (1964) AND NOT INAPPROPRIATE REGARDING ELVIS AND ANN-MARGRET'S SIZZLING CHEMISTRY ON AND OFFSCREEN. THE TWO REPORTEDLY DISCUSSED MARRIAGE BUT HE INSISTED SHE GIVE UP HER CAREER.

◀ APPRECIATION: THE ROMANCE BETWEEN ANN-MARGRET (SEEN HERE SINGING "APPRECIATION" IN **VIVA LAS VEGAS**, 1964) AND ELVIS TURNED INTO A LIFELONG FRIENDSHIP. SHE WROTE, "I TREASURE THE TIME WE WERE TOGETHER AND I FEEL LUCKY AND FULFILLED THAT WE WERE ABLE TO SUSTAIN SUCH A LONG, LOVING, AND CARING RELATIONSHIP."

◀ INITIALLY, ELVIS'S HOLLYWOOD MOVIES
WERE INTERNATIONAL HITS, FOR INSTANCE
ROUSTABOUT (1964), WHOSE ITALIAN TITLE
WAS *IL CANTANTE DEL LUNA PARK* (THE
SINGER FROM LUNA PARK).

▲ HAREM DOESN'T SCARE 'IM: ELVIS GOES
MIDEASTERN IN *HARUM SCARUM* (1965). IN
REAL LIFE, PRESLEY BASICALLY HAD A HAREM
BEFORE, DURING, AND AFTER MARRIAGE. HE
BELIEVED IN MONOGAMY—FOR WOMEN.

▲ ELVIS WAS RECREATED IN RUDOLPH
VALENTINO'S SILENT-ERA "SHEIK" IMAGE
IN *HARUM SCARUM* (1965) BUT FELT "SILLY
WEARING A TABLECLOTH" (THE UK TITLE,
HAREM HOLIDAY, SPELLED THE WORD
CORRECTLY).

▶ PROMOTIONAL SHOT FOR *GIRL HAPPY* (1965).
CELEBRITY PHOTOGRAPHER RICHARD AVEDON
FELT, "ELVIS WAS CONFIDENT IN HIS LOOKS
BUT NOT OVERLY FOND OF POSING. . . . HE
DIDN'T WANT TO BE JUST A SEX SYMBOL OR
HAVE A FOCUS ON HIS CHEST OR PELVIS—HE
HATED BEING CALLED ELVIS THE PELVIS."

▲ IN *SPINOUT* (1966) AND *SPEEDWAY* (1968) ELVIS
RACED CARS. A FAN OF JAMES DEAN, WHO DIED
IN A CAR CRASH IN 1955, PRESLEY WAS QUOTED,
"I LOVE CARS AND I LIKE SPEED BUT I CAN THINK
OF BETTER WAYS TO GO THAN TRAPPED INSIDE A
SMASHED-UP PIECE OF METAL."

► CHOICES, CHOICES: ELVIS MUST CHOOSE
BETWEEN THREE BUT YOUNG WOMEN WHO
PURSUE HIM AS AN IRRESISTIBLE SINGER
IN **SPINOUT** (1966), ONE OF FEW PRESLEY
VEHICLES THAT HAD ANY AUTOBIOGRAPHICAL
REFERENCES.

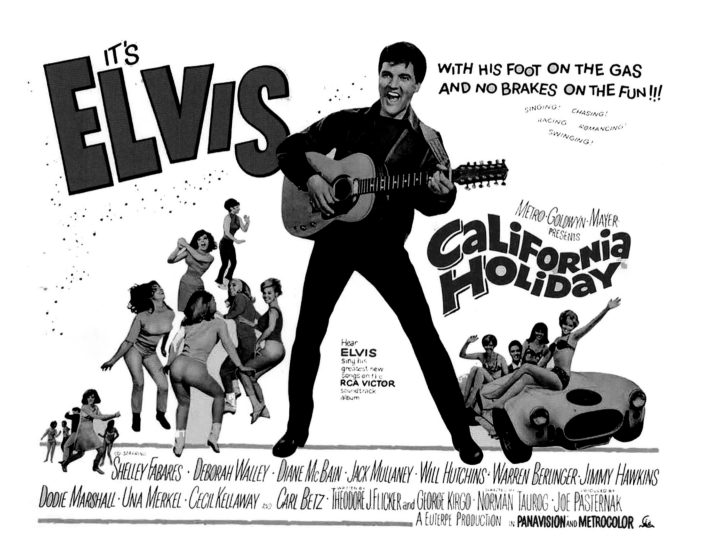

▼ ELVIS PLAYED A NAVY FROGMAN IN *EASY COME, EASY GO* (1967). COSTAR ELSA LANCHESTER—TOP OF POSTER—REVEALED, "MR. PRESLEY HAD DONE OVER TWENTY PICTURES BY THAT TIME AND DIDN'T WISH TO LINGER ANY LONGER THAN NEED BE . . . HE WAS ALWAYS EAGER TO DEPART."

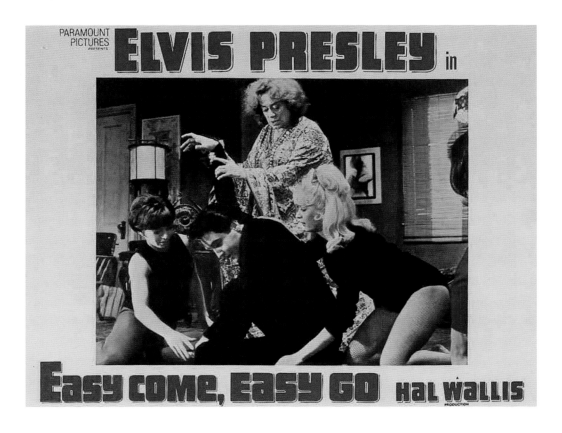

▼ ELVIS GREW INCREASINGLY DISSATISFIED WITH HIS HOKEY, FORMULAIC FILMS. OF **DOUBLE TROUBLE** (1967) HE FUMED, "YOU MEAN IT'S COME TO THIS? THOSE DAMN FOOLS GOT ME SINGING 'OLD MACDONALD' ON THE BACK OF A TRUCK WITH A BUNCH OF ANIMALS. MAN, IT'S A JOKE AND THE JOKE'S ON ME."

Part 3: The Icon

In Switzerland it's illegal to mow one's front lawn dressed as Elvis Presley (apparently anything goes in one's backyard). A sect called the First Presleyterian Church of the Divine Elvis was founded in the USA. One of the most popular Mexican-American live performers is El Vez, "the Mexican Elvis," with and without his backup singers, The Lovely Elvettes and The Memphis Mariachis. Japan still has more Elvis fan clubs than any country but his own and the UK.

To many then and now, Elvis is the essence of cool. His looks and musical impact, his barely suppressed sexual energy, his standing apart from other singers continue to win him fans globally. His records still sell; his appeal endures in his music. He began as a pre-famous youth who traveled town to town to sing on stage. The tail of his career took him back to his roots: a super-famous man traveling town to town singing his songs and offering himself up as a spectacle.

Despite his image of being cool, confident, and cocky, Elvis harbored a streak of insecurity and fear of being laughed at. During his earliest performances, when audiences hooted and made themselves heard, he thought they disliked him or were making fun of him. In time he realized audiences were going wild over him.

Thanks to his thirty-one Hollywood movies the star mostly lost touch with audiences—his voice and style were no longer live or truly Elvis. Rather, his pasteurized singing was used to record bland songs to sell movie-soundtrack albums and films of less and less interest. Priscilla Presley revealed that his 1968 filmed-for-TV performance comeback gave him "a shot of self-esteem he sorely needed. He'd been down on himself for so long." As she put it, his return to performing smashed "the barrier of mediocrity built up by so many forgettable movies."

Elvis admitted, "For nearly ten years I have been kept away from the public, and the one thing I loved was performing. But I'm not sure they're gonna like me now."

One reason Elvis's musical material became so second-rate through most of the '60s was that his manager the Colonel demanded that songwriters sign over a percentage of their publishing rights for any song Presley recorded. Virtually no top songwriter would consider such an arrangement.

Because Elvis's movie income had dipped markedly, the Colonel sanctioned what was to be a 1968 Christmas TV special (and accompanying album). He planned for Elvis to come out, say, "Good evening, ladies and gentlemen," sing twenty-six Christmas songs, then say, "Merry Christmas and good night." But Elvis and the show's young director Steve Binder wanted something more hip, more real-Elvis. More like the young man of the 1950s, including the soon-to-be-iconic black leather suit.

When he donned the suit Elvis told his wife he felt "a little silly in this thing." She replied he'd never looked better. Brooding in the makeup chair, sweating, he told his attendants, "I haven't been in front of those people in eight years. What am I gonna do if they don't like me? What if they laugh at me?"

The 1968 TV special *Elvis* was not only a big success, it turned Elvis's career around. *Eye* critic Jon Landau observed, "There is something magical about watching a man who has lost himself find his way home."

Presley began paying less heed to Col. Parker's taste and dictates. In January 1969 he entered a Memphis recording studio for the first time since leaving Sun Records. He announced that he didn't care "what the deal is, I don't care about publishing . . . I just want some great material." Elvis's musical comeback was cemented with "Suspicious Minds," his first number-one hit song in seven years.

The Colonel negotiated a month-long contract with the huge yet-to-be-built International Hotel in Las Vegas—Elvis's first public appearance in over eight years—for a July 31, 1969, debut. But Presley wouldn't inaugurate the International's 2,000-seat showroom, Vegas's largest. New superstar Barbra Streisand would. Parker didn't want that extra psychological burden for his client; Elvis still remembered his unsuccessful Las Vegas debut in 1956. Besides watching Streisand perform he now closely studied local-hot-ticket competitor Tom Jones.

When Elvis's International engagement proved a smash success the Colonel foresaw a money-guaranteed future of live performances. The fact that Elvis sold out every show despite working seven nights a week and two shows a night warmed the cockles of Tom Parker's heart, never mind the mental and physical—and eventually pharmacological—strain of such intense and sustained performing. ✳

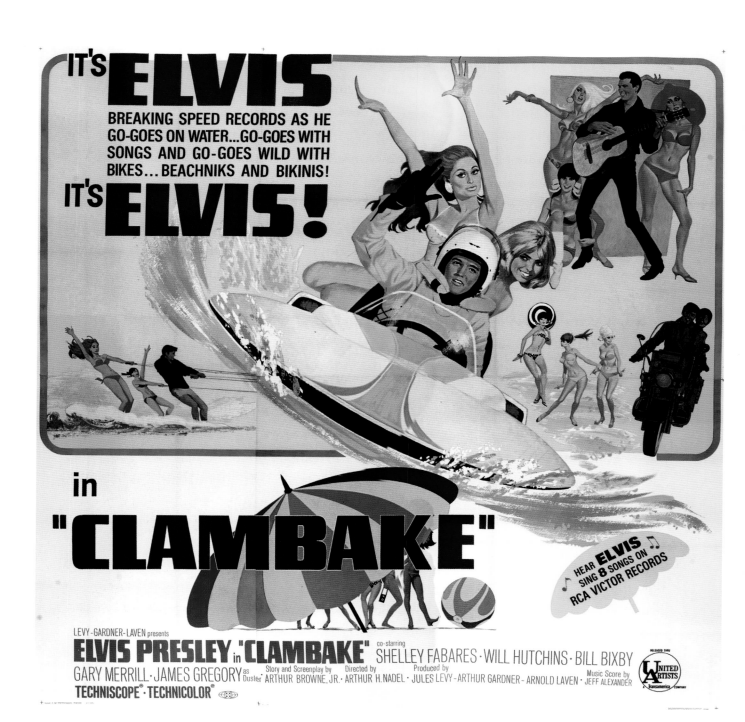

▼ POSSIBLY THE WORLD'S MOST DESIRED BACHELOR
FINALLY MARRIED AT THIRTY-TWO AT THE
ALADDIN HOTEL IN LAS VEGAS ON MAY 1, 1967, IN
A CEREMONY ORCHESTRATED BY THE COLONEL.
PRISCILLA LATER WROTE THAT IT WASN'T THE
WEDDING SHE'D DREAMED OF, BUT BOTH PARTIES
LET ELVIS'S MANAGER HAVE HIS WAY.

◄ *CLAMBAKE* (1967), ITS POSTER STRONGLY
INFLUENCED BY JAMES BOND, WAS ONE OF
NUMEROUS PRESLEY VEHICLES WITH A SEASIDE
SETTING. ELVIS WAS ONLY MODERATELY FOND OF
SWIMMING BUT HAD A GUITAR-SHAPED POOL.

▼ IN 1957, PARTLY TO AFFORD HIS FAMILY MORE PRIVACY, ELVIS BOUGHT GRACELAND, A MANSION ON THE OUTSKIRTS OF MEMPHIS NAMED AFTER THE GREAT-AUNT OF THE WOMAN IT WAS BUILT FOR. THE FOURTEEN-ACRE PROPERTY COST $102,500, AT A TIME WHEN THE AVERAGE ANNUAL AMERICAN WAGE WAS $3,641.72.

▲ **ELVIS'S SPEEDWAY** (1968) COSTAR WAS NANCY
SINATRA, WHOSE FATHER HAD STRONGLY
CRITICIZED ROCK 'N ROLL AND ELVIS PRESLEY IN
THE 1950S BUT DID AN ABOUT-FACE WHEN HE
WELCOMED ELVIS, POST-ARMY, ONTO HIS MAY
1960 FRANK SINATRA TELEVISION SPECIAL.

► ELVIS CONCLUDED HIS 1968 TELEVISION
SPECIAL *ELVIS* WITH THE SONG "IF I CAN
DREAM." THIS IMAGE BECAME THE COVER OF
THE RECORD ALBUM OF THE SHOW.

ELVIS TOLD THE PRODUCER OF HIS 1968 COMEBACK TV SPECIAL, "FOR NEARLY TEN YEARS I HAVE BEEN KEPT AWAY FROM THE PUBLIC, AND THE ONE THING I LOVED WAS PERFORMING. BUT I'M NOT SURE THEY'RE GONNA LIKE ME NOW." IN OR OUT OF BLACK LEATHER, HE WAS WRONG.

CHARRO (1969), A WESTERN SET IN MEXICO, HAD ONLY ONE SONG AND ELVIS WORE STUBBLE FOR THE FIRST TIME ONSCREEN. THE FILM WAS A CALCULATED CHANGE OF IMAGE BUT TOO LATE—PRESLEY'S ACTING CAREER ENDED LATER THAT YEAR.

On his neck he wore the brand of a killer. On his hip he wore vengeance.

National General Pictures presents

ELVIS PRESLEY as CHARRO!

A different kind of role.
A different kind of man.

Co-starring INA BALIN · VICTOR FRENCH · BARBARA WERLE · SOLOMON STURGES

and introducing LYNN KELLOGG Executive Producer Harry Caplan Produced and Directed by Charles Marquis Warren Screenplay by Charles Marquis Warren Story by Frederic Louis Fox Music Composed and Conducted by Hugo Montenegro

[G] Suggested for GENERAL Audiences "Charro!" sung by Elvis Presley on RCA Records TECHNICOLOR® PANAVISION® *A NEW EXCITEMENT IN ENTERTAINMENT*

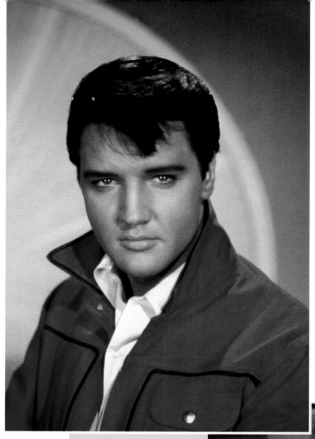

◀ PRE-1970S ELVIS DIDN'T WEAR RHINESTONES AND SELDOM WORE RINGS. SEVENTIES ELVIS HAD TO WEAR BAND-AIDS ON HIS FINGERS WHILE PERFORMING TO PREVENT FANS PULLING OFF HIS RINGS. WHEN FANS CHOSE WHICH ELVIS SHOULD BE ON THE 1993 TWENTY-NINE-CENT STAMP THEY VOTED FOR '50S ELVIS OVER VEGAS ELVIS.

▼ INCREDIBLE: ELVIS PLAYED A DOCTOR AND MARY TYLER MOORE AND SINGER BARBARA MCNAIR PLAYED NUNS IN HIS CHANGE-OF-PACE (SOME SAID FROM DESPERATION) MOVIE *CHANGE OF HABIT* (1969). IT WAS HIS FINAL MOVIE.

▲ ELVIS MADE HIS LIVE-PERFORMANCE COMEBACK
AT THE INTERNATIONAL HOTEL IN LAS VEGAS
IN SUMMER 1969 WHERE HE PERFORMED
FOR FOUR WEEKS, THE FIRST OF NUMEROUS
EXTENDED HOTEL DATES.

◀ PRISCILLA PRESLEY REVEALED, "UNEXPECTEDLY, THE BIRTH OF [DAUGHTER LISA MARIE IN 1968], WHICH I REASONED WOULD BRING MY HUSBAND AND MYSELF CLOSER TOGETHER, PUSHED US APART. ELVIS AVOIDED INTIMACY WITH ME. I REMEMBER HIM TELLING ME SOME TIME IN THE PAST THAT HE JUST COULDN'T HAVE SEX WITH A WOMAN WHO'D HAD A CHILD."

▲ MOTHER PRISCILLA SAID ELVIS SPOILED THEIR DAUGHTER, SPANKING HER ONCE EVER AND ALMOST NEVER RAISING HIS VOICE TO HER, LET ALONE SHOUTING—"ELVIS WAS HORRIFIED AT WHAT HE HAD DONE. HIS SCOLDING WAS FAR MORE TRAUMATIC FOR HIM THAN HER."

▶ IN SEPTEMBER 1970 WHEN ELVIS EMBARKED ON HIS FIRST TOUR SINCE 1957 HE WORRIED THAT HIS (NOT-YET-GAUDY) STAGE COSTUMES MIGHT BE LAUGHED AT. BUT AS THE SARTORIALLY FLAMBOYANT '70S WORE ON, HE NO LONGER WORRIED—ELVIS PERFORMED OVER 1,000 SHOWS BETWEEN 1970 AND 1977.

▲ ELVIS SHED HIS PUPPY FAT OF THE 1950S AND '60S AND WAS AT HIS MOST CHISELED AFTER HOLLYWOOD, TOWARD THE START OF HIS LIVE-PERFORMING COMEBACK.

▶ ELVIS CONSIDERED BLACK HAIR MORE MASCULINE THAN HIS OWN DARK BLOND AND ADOPTED IT EARLY ON (WIFE PRISCILLA DYED HERS BLACK TOO). LIKE HIS FATHER, ELVIS'S HAIR WENT PREMATURELY WHITE— PERSONAL HAIRDRESSER LARRY GELLER SUGGESTED HE GO "SILVER-HAIRED;" ELVIS SAID HE'D "GIVE IT SOME THOUGHT" (SHORTLY BEFORE HIS DEATH AT FORTY-TWO).

▲ ELVIS, 1970S-STYLE, WOULD GIVE RISE TO AN ARMY OF IMPERSONATORS. PRISCILLA PRESLEY ADMITTED, "THE JUMPSUITS AND CAPES WOULD GET EXCESSIVE, BUT [AT THE START] THEY ESTABLISHED HIS NEW IDENTITY AND HELPED GIVE HIM CONFIDENCE."

▶ *ELVIS: THAT'S THE WAY IT IS* (1970, RELEASED SHORTLY BEFORE CHRISTMAS) WAS HIS FIRST SCREEN EFFORT SINCE GIVING UP ACTING THE YEAR BEFORE. THE DOCUMENTARY FOLLOWED HIM THROUGH DAYS OF INTENSIVE PREPARATION FOR HIS LAS VEGAS SHOW TO HIS ECSTATICALLY RECEIVED OPENING NIGHT AT THE INTERNATIONAL HOTEL, PERFORMING TWENTY-SEVEN SONGS.

▶ IN EARLY 1970 ELVIS BEGAN WEARING ONE-PIECE JUMPSUITS, WHICH ALLOWED FOR GREATER FREEDOM OF MOVEMENT, INCLUDING HIS KARATE-INSPIRED POSES. INITIALLY ALL-WHITE OR ALL-BLACK, THEY WERE CREATED BY I.C. (ICE CAPADES) COSTUMES IN LOS ANGELES.

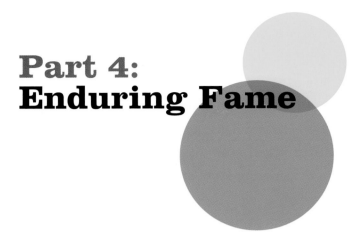

Part 4:
Enduring Fame

Fame usually brings fortune and adulation, though financial freedom comes with certain social restraints. When Elvis Presley hit back at a gas station owner who assaulted him minus provocation, the new star found himself in a courtroom and a national spotlight. Numerous lawsuits would trail Elvis over the decades, and female adulation could incite active male jealousy. After one 1955 performance in Lubbock, Texas, Elvis was beckoned by a man in a car. The singer got close enough for the driver to punch him in the face and speed off.

Bodyguards became essential not only for concerts but daily life. Elvis's guards, gofers, and hangers-on became known as the Memphis Mafia and shared his background. When Elvis went to Hollywood he met a more educated and sophisticated set but felt insecure around them. In his sixth-grade class photo he was the only child wearing overalls. The feeling of not measuring up stayed with him. Elvis eventually bought a mansion in Los Angeles but never considered it home. He shunned celebrity company, preferring to be the star among his down-home peers.

Since Elvis grew up before the peacock revolution of the 1960s and '70s it wasn't until his Las Vegas period that he began wearing lots of jewelry and ostentatious stage outfits. That new-look Elvis would spawn generations of Elvis impersonators and made a ton of money, however, many fans missed the original Elvis—the king of rock 'n roll before he broadened his musical horizons and was tamed for the big screen. Significantly, when fans were asked to vote for which Elvis should appear on commemorative stamps in 1993 and 2015 they chose the original one.

Presley's national impact may be measured by the file the FBI accumulated on him, running to over six-hundred pages. The original Elvis was considered dangerous by many in authority, from parents and preachers to J. Edgar Hoover, who deemed him "immoral" and a "menace." Elvis would have been amazed. He knew he was pushing the boundaries of on-stage sexiness yet was himself rather shy, even prudish. He bristled at the nickname "Elvis the Pelvis" and declined to pose for beefcake fan photos. He also endured the widespread opinion that Elvis the golden goose was under the greedy thumb of his domineering manager the "Colonel."

However, Col. Parker and the media did a necessary job of covering up for twenty-four-year-old Elvis when he was dating a fourteen-year-old who much later became his wife, plus his myriad sexual escapades before and during the marriage. The shocking amount of drugs Elvis took was also a longtime secret, though their origin was far from scandalous: insomnia. Elvis's lengthy Las Vegas engagements and concert tours escalated his drug usage. Some lent him confidence, for though he felt at home on stage he experienced occasional panic attacks before a show. After a show his adrenalin had to be diminished to allow him to sleep.

Elvis suffered two tragedies that cast a long shadow. The 1958 death of his mother Gladys at forty-six left him inconsolable (the Presleys weren't long-lived; father Vernon died in 1979 at sixty-three). When Vern remarried in 1960 Elvis refused to attend the wedding. The psychological bond between mother and son had been such that in later life Elvis eschewed sex with females who were mothers, as ex wife Priscilla Beaulieu Presley has confirmed.

The second tragedy was the inevitable break-up of his 1967 marriage, with a legal separation in 1972 and divorce in '73. All the more so when Priscilla and daughter Lisa Marie moved out of Elvis's home at Graceland for good.

His final years saw an increase in such drug-fueled erratic behavior as getting mad at a guitar and throwing it into a concert audience, shooting at television sets, ordering an underling in 1973 to kill karate instructor Mike Stone because Priscilla had fallen in love with him, giggling on stage and forgetting lyrics, or in 1976 announcing during a Las Vegas show, "I hate Las Vegas."

A clear sign of the beginning of the end was when Elvis, always quietly proud of his looks, let himself start gaining weight. In the 1950s he reportedly had surgery to thin his nose and he began the lifelong dyeing of his hair black, a more "macho" color he felt secure with. In July 1975 he had cosmetic surgery around his eyes, against the advice of his personal physician and the plastic surgeon. When he'd turned forty that year he spent the day secluded in his bedroom. The public didn't know that his hair, like his father's before him, had turned prematurely white.

Regardless, his public stood by Elvis, and with his early death ageing and his downward spiral ceased and he became more popular than ever and was re-evaluated as a cultural phenomenon. His charisma transcended death and kept music sales and interest in the man alive. Graceland became a popular tourist and pilgrimage site. Whichever version of Elvis one chooses to remember, the music and the magnetism of the one and only, rule-breaking Elvis Presley endure. *

▲ **THIS IS ELVIS** (1981) WAS A POSTHUMOUS DOCUMENTARY FILM THAT INCLUDED HOME MOVIES, CONCERT FOOTAGE, AND DRAMATIZATIONS. THE LATTER WERE ROUNDLY CRITICIZED BY MOST REVIEWERS.

▼ DURING LIVE PERFORMANCES ELVIS GAVE AWAY HUNDREDS OF SCARVES TO INDIVIDUAL FEMALE FANS WHO TREASURED THE MEMENTO. MANY, PERHAPS MOST, SUCH SCARVES ARE SAID NEVER TO HAVE BEEN WASHED.

▲ ELVIS'S APRIL 1972 CONCERTS WERE FILMED
FOR THE DOCUMENTARY *ELVIS ON TOUR*
(1973).

▲ ELVIS, WHO REMOVED HIS BIG-BUCKLED BELT
EARLIER DURING THE SHOW, IN *ELVIS ON TOUR*
(1973), HIS SECOND AND FINAL DOCUMENTARY
FILM SINCE RETIRING FROM ACTING IN 1969. IT
CAPTURED HIS NATIONAL CONCERT TOUR AND
OFFERED "A TOUR OF ELVIS'S LIFE, A CLOSE-UP
OF THE BIRTH AND LIFE OF AN AMERICAN
PHENOMENON."

▼ POST-DIVORCE, ELVIS AND PRISCILLA REMAINED—
OR MORE ACCURATELY, BECAME—FRIENDS,
AND ELVIS OFTEN SOUGHT HER ADVICE. SHE
HELPED CHOOSE THE OUTSIZED BELT BUCKLES
THAT BECAME AN INTEGRAL PART OF HIS STAGE
WARDROBE.

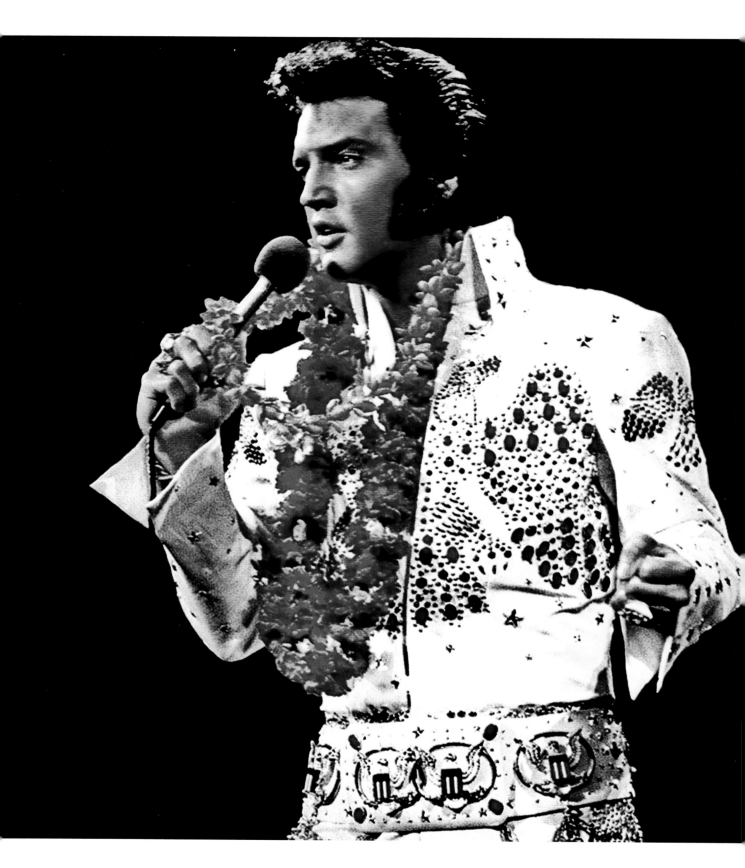

◄ ELVIS'S *ALOHA FROM HAWAII*, VIA SATELLITE TV
SPECIAL WAS TAPED IN HONOLULU ON JANUARY
14, 1973, AND BROADCAST LIVE THROUGH
MUCH OF AUSTRALASIA. WHEN IT AIRED ON US
TELEVISION ON APRIL 4 SOME FIFTY-ONE PERCENT
OF THE VIEWING AUDIENCE TUNED IN.

▲ A 1973 STUTZ BLACKHAWK WAS THE LAST CAR
ELVIS EVER DROVE, LESS THAN TWELVE HOURS
BEFORE HIS 1977 DEATH. ITS INTERIOR WAS RED
LEATHER WITH 18-KARAT GOLD-PLATED TRIM—
ELVIS BOUGHT IT IN 1974 FOR $20,000.

▲ BOBBY "RED" WEST AND ELVIS DURING A FILMED EXHIBITION ON SEPTEMBER 16, 1974, AT THE TENNESSEE KARATE INSTITUTE. WEST BECAME A LIFELONG FRIEND AND SOMETIME BODYGUARD TO PRESLEY AFTER THE FOOTBALL PLAYER DEFENDED HIM IN SCHOOL WHEN A GROUP OF BOYS CORNERED ELVIS AND THREATENED TO CUT HIS HAIR.

▶ ELVIS'S FAVORITE COLORS WERE BLACK AND PINK. DURING HIS POST-MOVIES LIVE-PERFORMING COMEBACK HE FAVORED BLACK, BUT AS HIS LAS VEGAS AND TOURING OUTFITS WENT FROM FLASHY TO FLAMBOYANT HE FOCUSED ON WHITE.

▲ GAUDY, BAWDY, AND OH LAWDY: AS
ELVIS GAINED WEIGHT (HERE IN CONCERT
IN JULY 1975 IN NORTH CAROLINA), SOME
ADVISORS URGED HIM TO TONE DOWN THE
COSTUMES—THIS ONE FEATURED BEADS
FROM THE KNEES DOWN—BUT ELVIS FELT
THEY WOULD DISTRACT FROM HIS GIRTH.

◀ ON STAGE, ELVIS LIKED TO MOVE AND STRIKE POSES, INCLUDING SOME INSPIRED BY KARATE. AFTER GAINING WEIGHT HE SOMETIMES POPPED BUTTONS OR SPLIT HIS SEAMS, JOKING WITH AUDIENCES THAT HE OUGHT TO CUT DOWN ON HIS CALORIES.

▶ ZAFTIG PRESLEY: IN CONCERT ON MAY 1, 1975, IN ATLANTA, GEORGIA. ELVIS WAS FAR MORE CONCERNED WITH HIS LOOKS IN THE 1950S, WHEN HE REPORTEDLY HAD PLASTIC SURGERY BECAUSE HE FELT HIS NOSE WAS TOO WIDE. WHILE IN THE ARMY IN GERMANY HE UNDERWENT WEEKLY TREATMENTS FROM A SPECIALIST IN ENLARGED PORES AND ACNE SCARS.

▲ CROWDS GATHER AT THE GATES OF GRACELAND ON AUGUST 17, 1977, DRAWN BY THE NEWS OF ELVIS PRESLEY'S DEATH. AN ESTIMATED 50,000 PEOPLE VIEWED ELVIS IN HIS OPEN COPPER CASKET, PRIOR TO THE NEXT DAY'S FUNERAL PROCESSION.

▼ ON AUGUST 18, 1977, A WHITE HEARSE FOLLOWED BY SEVENTEEN WHITE LIMOUSINES BEARS ELVIS PRESLEY'S BODY FROM GRACELAND TO THE MEMPHIS CEMETERY WHERE HIS MOTHER GLADYS IS BURIED. ON OCTOBER 2 THEIR BODIES WERE TRANSFERRED TO THE MEDITATION GARDEN AT GRACELAND.

▲ THE RACQUETBALL BUILDING AT GRACELAND IS USED TO SHOWCASE MORE OF ELVIS'S OUTFITS, GOLD RECORDS, AND MUSIC AWARDS. OVER 600,000 PEOPLE A YEAR VISIT ELVIS'S FORMER HOME AND FINAL RESTING PLACE.

A MEDITATION GARDEN WAS BUILT BEHIND GRACELAND IN THE MID 1960S AS A PRIVATE OUTDOOR REFUGE FOR ELVIS. THE MEDITATION GARDEN IS NOW THE PRESLEY BURIAL GROUND AND INCLUDES ELVIS, MOTHER GLADYS, FATHER VERNON, GRANDMOTHER MINNIE MAE PRESLEY, AND OTHER FAMILY MEMBERS.

▼ GRACELAND BY NIGHT: BUILT IN 1939, THE SITE
IS ON THE NATIONAL REGISTER OF HISTORIC
PLACES BUT UPON ELVIS'S DEATH IN 1977
WAS AT RISK OF BEING SOLD TO PAY ITS BILLS.
EX WIFE PRISCILLA PRESLEY, MOTHER AND
GUARDIAN OF HEIRESS LISA MARIE PRESLEY,
DECIDED THE BEST WAY TO SAVE THE HOUSE
WAS TO INVITE THE PAYING PUBLIC IN—IT
OPENED ON JUNE 7, 1982.